B1 Writing

Cambridge Masterclass

Margaret Cooze

© Prosperity Education Ltd. 2023

Registered offices: Sherlock Close, Cambridge
CB3 0HP, United Kingdom

First published 2023

ISBN: 978-1-913825-79-9

This publication is in copyright. Subject to statutory exception
and to the provisions of relevant collective licensing agreements,
no reproduction of any part may take place without the written
permission of Prosperity Education.

The moral right of the author has been asserted.

'Cambridge B1 Preliminary' and 'PET' are brands
belonging to The Chancellor, Masters and Scholars of the
University of Cambridge and are not associated with
Prosperity Education or its products.

Designed by ORP Cambridge

For further information and resources, visit:
www.prosperityeducation.net

To infinity and beyond.

Contents

Introduction 5

Task type **1. Email** 17

Task type **2. Article** 33

Task type **3. Story** 49

Practice tests 65

Margaret Cooze holds an MA in Applied Linguistics and an MSc in English Language Teaching Management, and has worked in senior roles at Cambridge English Language Assessment and Cambridge Assessment International Education. She is the author of several ELT resources published by Cambridge University Press.

Introduction

Cambridge B1 Preliminary Writing

Welcome to this book on the Cambridge B1 Preliminary Writing paper. B1 Preliminary is one of the exams in the series provided by Cambridge Assessment – part of the University of Cambridge. It is the second in the range of tests they provide in General English:

A2	Key (KET)
B1	Preliminary (PET)
B2	First (FCE)
C1	Advanced (CAE)
C2	Proficiency (CPE)

The references next to each test refer to the CEFR Level (Common European Framework of Reference), and show the language level of each test.

For CEFR B1 Writing, you will be able to:

- communicate your ideas in writing on everyday topics

- write clearly and in some detail

- explain your ideas about a situation

- recognise the reader of texts and use a suitable register

- show different grammatical structures

- show suitable vocabulary for the tasks set

- recognise the functional language needed in tasks.

How does the test work?

You can take the B1 Preliminary exam on a computer or on paper. The content is the same for both forms of the test. The B1 Preliminary Writing paper gives you the opportunity to show your language skills. The topics of tasks are chosen so that they are relevant to the typical student taking this exam, so you should find that you have enough ideas to write about. Each question will guide you by identifying the context, the purpose for writing and the target reader. It is important to remember that you aren't being tested on the subject content of the tasks. So, if the topic of the Part 1 question, for example, is education, you aren't expected to be an expert about this topic. The test format is:

Time allowed	45 minutes
Number of parts	2
Number of questions	Part 1: one compulsory question Part 2: one optional question from a choice of two
Task types	essay, article, story
Length	each answer should be about 100 words long

Task type 1: Email

Part 1 (Question 1) of the Writing paper is always an email written in reply to an email you have been sent. There will be four 'notes' on the side of the email that will guide you in writing your email in reply.

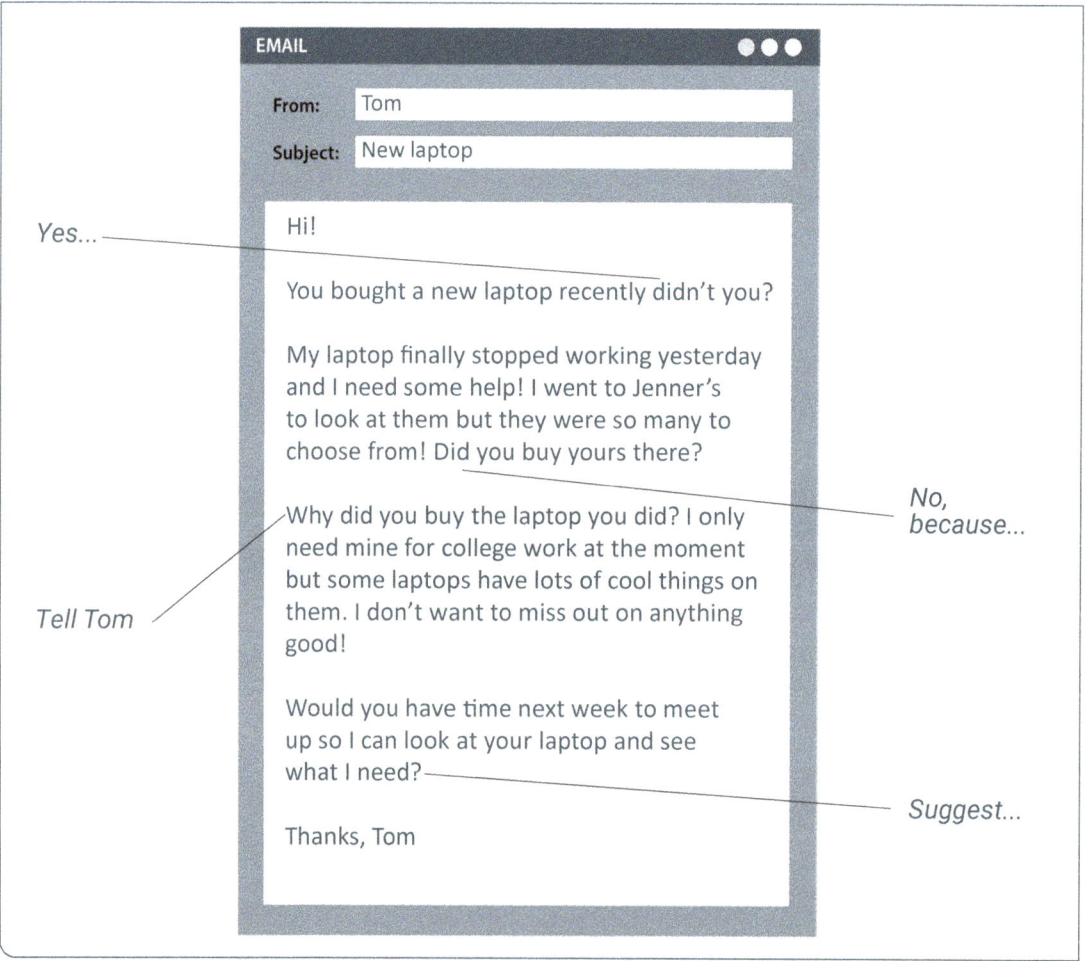

Introduction

You must include information for each of the notes provided, and this will be made clear in the question. For example:

> Read this email from your English-speaking friend Tom and the notes you have made.
>
> Write your **email** to Tom using **all the notes**.

It's a good idea to tick these off on the question paper as you include them to make sure that you don't miss anything. You can get used to thinking about these notes by recognising what you are expected to do.

Look at these examples:

Email content	Note	What you need to do
Shall we go to football?	*Great idea!*	Agree that this is a good idea (but try to use different words).
Shall we go to football?	*No, because…*	Here you need to disagree with the writer and say why you disagree.

As you can see, the same content in the email might have different notes, so it's very important that you think about what the notes are telling you to do.

Here are some more examples of notes:

Email content	Note	What you need to do
We could go for pizza or eat at my house.	*Tell Maria…*	Tell Maria which of the two options is best.
Have I forgotten anything?	*Yes…*	Tell the writer that they have forgotten something, and say what it is. You can't say that they haven't forgotten anything with this note.
I don't know where to go in the evening.	*Suggest…*	Make a suggestion of a place the writer could go.
If you have any questions, let me know.	*Ask Mrs Jenkins…*	You need to ask a question that is relevant to the email content here.

An email can be organised in different ways, and some of the notes can be covered quickly while others will need more words to reply. Emails to a friend may be less formal, and emails to a teacher should be semi-formal and polite. Remember, you don't have to tell the truth! The examiners won't know, so if you don't have experience or an opinion you can make something up.

Task type 2: Article

An article is usually written for an English-language magazine or website. Therefore, the reader will have a similar background to you.

> **Articles wanted!**
>
> **What do you do to keep healthy?**
>
> Is thinking about what you eat more important than how much you exercise?
> What are your recommendations for keeping healthy?
>
> The best articles will be published on our website in our health feature next month.

Imagine a group of your friends reading your article. An article should have some opinion or comment that the reader will be interested in reading. A title is useful to attract attention, and it's good to try to give a strong ending to leave the reader with something to think about. The grammar and vocabulary that you need for an article will depend on the question. Look at the examples in this book on pages 33 and 41. The first one could be written in the present tense (you could use other tenses too), but the second one definitely needs to be written in the past tense. The vocabulary will also depend on the question, and you should think about what good vocabulary you know for the topic.

Task type 3: Story

A story is usually written for a teacher. The question will give you a sentence to begin your story with. It's a good idea to underline or highlight the important words that will make sure your story fits with this sentence. For example:

This tells you that it is a girl in the story, so remember to use the right pronouns: she, her, hers.

This tells you that she didn't leave the key in the grass. Think about what she did with it, where she went, etc.

<u>Kate</u> saw a gold <u>key</u> in the <u>grass</u> and she <u>picked it up</u>.

This tells you the object. You should think about what the key is for and how Kate felt when she saw it.

This tells you where the key was – maybe a park or the countryside. This will help with the setting for your story.

Remember that your story needs to be linked with the ideas in the sentence in the question, but you aren't being tested on your creative writing – the story doesn't need to be exciting. You only have about 100 words to write your story, so it is best to keep your ideas simple.

You will need to use past tenses in a story, and the best B1 Preliminary stories use a range of different tenses: past simple, past continuous and past perfect. If you decide to choose the story question in the exam, think about how confident you are with this grammar. Good stories also use a range of different time phrases to link ideas. For example: then, afterwards, later that day, in the end, etc. These help to make a story easy to read.

How to use this book

The main section of this book focuses on each task type individually, explaining its characteristics and providing guidance on how to plan a response to an example question.

There are two example questions for each task type. For each task-type question, two responses from different candidates are provided. One response is very good and the other is less good, identifying areas that the candidate could improve on. There are detailed comments on each response, and a breakdown of the marks that the response could get in the exam. You should read these responses and commentary before you write your own response to the question. When you have written your response, look back at the comments and the mark scheme, and think about what you did well and also how you could have done better.

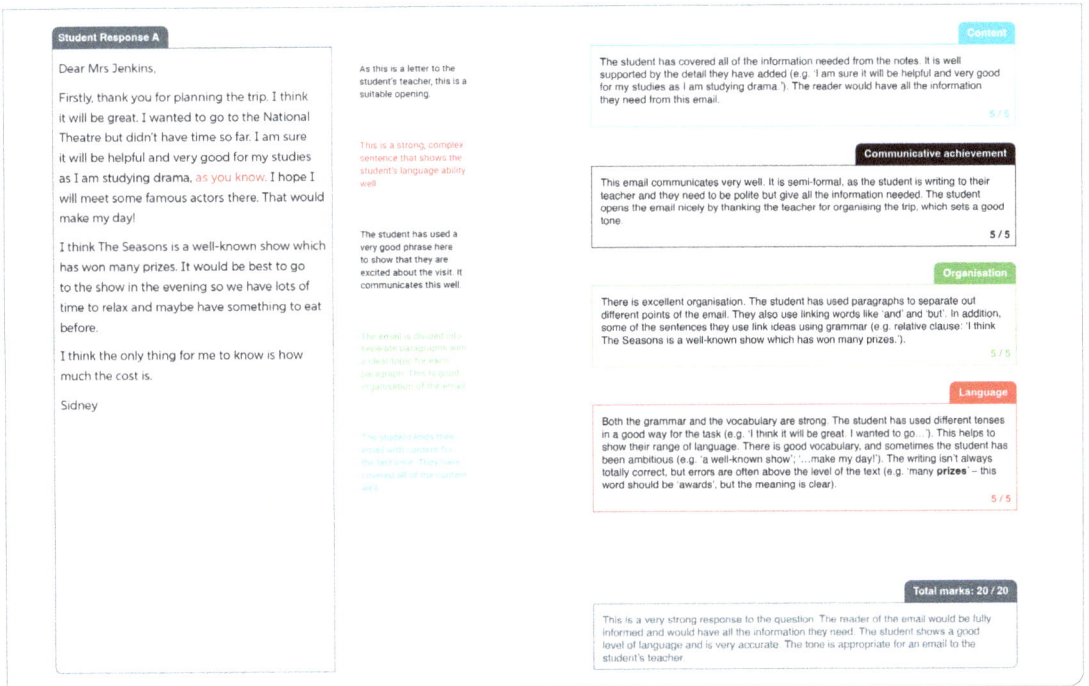

Preparing for the exam

It is important that you plan your time in the exam. You will need to complete both tasks within the 45 minutes.

It is sensible to divide your time equally between the two tasks: about 20 minutes each. You should make sure that you:

- **Read** all of the questions carefully to be certain you understand what they mean.
- **Plan** your writing.
- **Write** your response according to your plan.
- **Check** your writing for errors.

Read the questions

Read the Part 1 question carefully, and make sure that you understand what each of the four notes refers to. Read both of the Part 2 questions. There will be two questions, and you will need to choose one. When making your choice, you will need to think about the task type, the topic and the language that you will need.

It is good advice to spend time thinking about each question before you start writing. If you start one question and then realise that you don't feel confident about the ideas or language you need, you may need to change question.

Plan your writing

It is tempting to start writing as soon as you decide what question to answer, but spending some time planning is very sensible.

Candidates plan their writing in different ways, but the following is an example of a plan for the story question on page 8:

Para 1: walking to school | do something more exciting!

Para 2: key to special box | bank | box full of gold coins | felt shaky | grabbed gold | ran

Para 3: bought big house | good life | scared money from criminal!

Here, the candidate has noted down some ideas and good vocabulary to use, and has decided what will go in each paragraph.

Write your response

Use your notes to assemble your ideas from your plan into a well-organised piece of writing with a suitable tone and good, accurate language. With good planning technique, this will be easier. Of course, you will also be thinking about the functions, grammar and vocabulary that you considered before you started to produce your plan. This is the best way to make sure that you show the examiner as much of your language ability as possible.

It is a useful skill to paraphrase language that you find in the task. So, if the task says 'Is it better to buy things online or visit shops?', you could answer by saying 'I think it's better to buy things online.' But it would be better to paraphrase and say something like 'In my opinion, shopping on the internet isn't as much fun as going to the high street or shopping mall'. You show the examiner that you know more language this way.

What language do you need?

There are three things to consider when you have read the questions. There is some overlap between them, but it is still a good idea to think about all three.

1. What functions does the task need?

For example, do you need to give your opinion, explain something or give a recommendation?

2. What grammar can you use in the task?

This may be linked to the functions of the question. For example, if you are asked to give a suggestion, you'll be able to use modal verbs (e.g. 'You could go to…').

However, often the grammar you use will be your choice. If you know that you are confident when using conditional sentences, for example, can you include one in your response? If you know that you don't feel confident about using relative clauses, how can you avoid trying to use one?

3. What vocabulary is related to the task topic and links in with the functions?

This will depend on the question and the topic, but you should think about what phrases you can use to make sure that there is variety. For example, it is better not to start each idea with 'I think…'. You could use 'In my opinion…' or 'My view is…' as alternatives to make sure that you show the examiner a good range of different phrases.

Other vocabulary that you decide to use will be related to the topic. If the task is set in a park, for example, what vocabulary (e.g. *playground*, *gate*, *café*, *children*, etc.) might be good to use?

You can also think about which words or phrases you want to use to link ideas together. Using linking devices (e.g. *and*, *but, however*, *on the other hand*, *as opposed to*, etc.) helps with the organisation of your writing and makes it easier for the reader to understand it.

Check your writing

You should always leave five minutes to read through each response you write. Check that you haven't left anything important out, but also check the language for errors. For example:

Have you used the right tenses? Are there any spelling errors?

It's a good idea to make your own checklist while you prepare for the B1 Preliminary Writing paper. It will help you to think about what to check for, and also to think about mistakes that you often make.

Here is a suggested checklist to use, but it's a good idea to add things that you know you sometimes make mistakes with. What would you add to this checklist?

✔ ✘

- [ ] Does your response cover all of the content points in the task?
- [ ] Is your response in the right style for the task type?
- [ ] Have you used the right register for the task?
- [ ] Have you used paragraphs to separate different ideas?
- [ ] Have you used linking devices correctly?
- [ ] Have you got a range of linking devices?
- [ ] Are all tenses correct?
- [ ] Have you used articles with nouns where needed?
- [ ] Are the prepositions correct?
- [ ] What about errors you've made in the past?

The assessment criteria

Each piece of writing is marked against four assessment criteria, each carrying a maximum of five marks.

Content

This criterion focuses on whether you have answered the question and whether the reader would have all the information they need. You must make sure that you identify what the question is asking you to do, and plan your answer so that you stay on the topic. In Part 1 there are four notes that you must cover. In Part 2 you must identify what you will need to write about from the questions.

Max. 5 marks

Communicative achievement

This criterion focuses on how well you communicate with the reader. This includes whether your writing is suitable for the task you are writing and that it also involves register. Register means whether your writing is more formal (e.g. writing for someone you don't know or your teacher) or less formal (e.g. writing for your classmates or a friend).

Max. 5 marks

Organisation

This criterion focuses on how your ideas are organised into paragraphs, if these are needed. It includes the use of discourse markers (e.g. *and*, *but*, *so* at a basic level; and *therefore*, *despite this* at a higher level). It also includes things like how pronouns are used to refer to nouns to avoid repetition. For example: 'He never liked school and hated going there.' In this sentence, using the word 'there' means that the student doesn't repeat the word 'school'.

Max. 5 marks

Language

This criterion focuses on vocabulary and grammar. It isn't just about using vocabulary and grammar without making mistakes. It also considers whether your writing uses more difficult grammar and more unusual words and phrases. It is sometimes hard to focus on both, and, of course, it's great if you don't make any mistakes! However, if this means that your language is very simple, it may mean that you can't get to the top marks here.

Max. 5 marks

When all four criteria have been assessed your total mark is given out of 20.

B1 Writing | Cambridge Masterclass

Planning Guide

Write the question you are going to answer below, and underline or highlight the important words that will help you to focus your response.

What **functions** does the task need?

What **grammar** could you use?

What **vocabulary** could you use?

Bring your ideas together in a plan, and think about the organisation and register you need.

- How many paragraphs do you need? How will you link ideas?
- Who is your reader? What is your relationship to them?
- Do you need to use more formal or more informal language?

Text type 1: Email

B1 Preliminary Writing

In Part 1 of the Writing paper you will have to write an email. **Remember:**

- You must include all four points from the notes.
- Think about how to use your own words instead of the words in the question email.
- Make sure that you identify the person the email is being written for.
- Think about how formal or informal your email should be.

Look at the following question. **Think about:**

- what you could be studying that could be linked to this theatre trip
- why an afternoon or evening would be better
- what question you could ask.

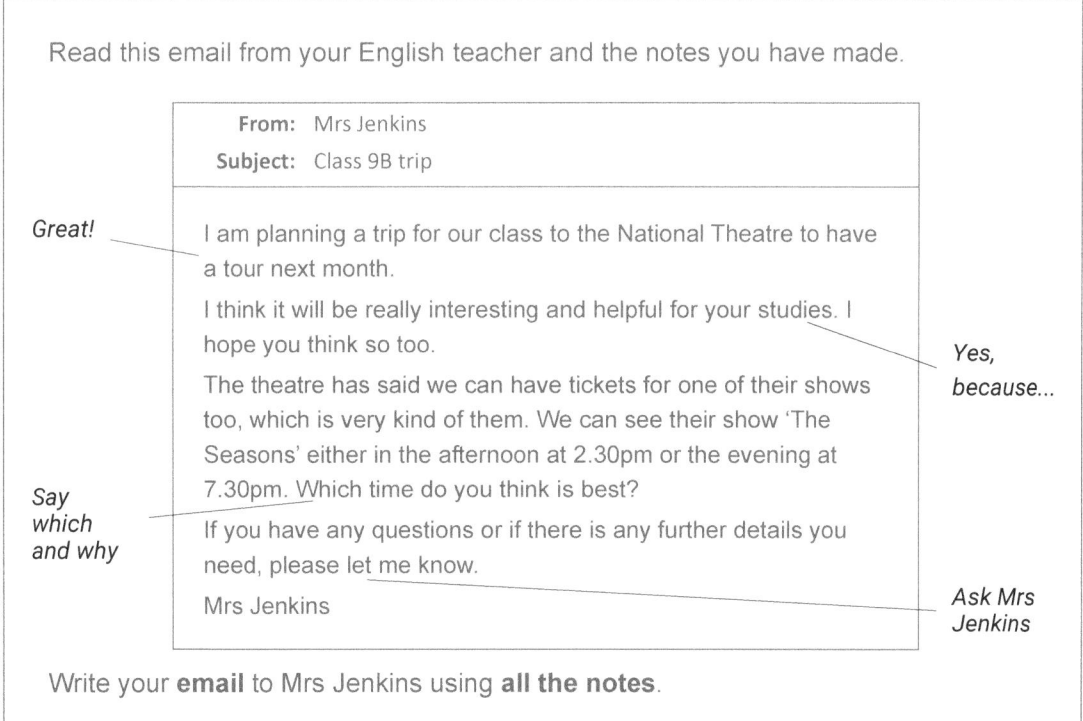

Read this email from your English teacher and the notes you have made.

From: Mrs Jenkins
Subject: Class 9B trip

Great!

I am planning a trip for our class to the National Theatre to have a tour next month.

I think it will be really interesting and helpful for your studies. I hope you think so too.

Yes, because...

The theatre has said we can have tickets for one of their shows too, which is very kind of them. We can see their show 'The Seasons' either in the afternoon at 2.30pm or the evening at 7.30pm. Which time do you think is best?

Say which and why

If you have any questions or if there is any further details you need, please let me know.

Mrs Jenkins

Ask Mrs Jenkins

Write your **email** to Mrs Jenkins using **all the notes**.

Read the following sample answers and see how two students have answered this task.

Student Response A

Dear Mrs Jenkins,

Firstly, thank you for planning the trip. I think it will be great. I wanted to go to the National Theatre but didn't have time so far. I am sure it will be helpful and very good for my studies as I am studying drama, as you know. I hope I will meet some famous actors there. That would make my day!

I think The Seasons is a well-known show which has won many prizes. It would be best to go to the show in the evening so we have lots of time to relax and maybe have something to eat before.

I think the only thing for me to know is how much the cost is.

Sidney

As this is a letter to the student's teacher, this is a suitable opening.

This is a strong, complex sentence that shows the student's language ability well.

The student has used a very good phrase here to show that they are excited about the visit. It communicates this well.

The email is divided into separate paragraphs with a clear topic for each paragraph. This is good organisation of the email.

The student ends their email with content for the last note. They have covered all of the content well.

Text type 1: Email

Content

The student has covered all of the information needed from the notes. It is well supported by the detail they have added (e.g. 'I am sure it will be helpful and very good for my studies as I am studying drama.'). The reader would have all the information they need from this email.

5 / 5

Communicative achievement

This email communicates very well. It is semi-formal, as the student is writing to their teacher and they need to be polite but give all the information needed. The student opens the email nicely by thanking the teacher for organising the trip, which sets a good tone.

5 / 5

Organisation

There is excellent organisation. The student has used paragraphs to separate out different points of the email. They also use linking words like 'and' and 'but'. In addition, some of the sentences they use link ideas using grammar (e.g. relative clause: 'I think The Seasons is a well-known show which has won many prizes.').

5 / 5

Language

Both the grammar and the vocabulary are strong. The student has used different tenses in a good way for the task (e.g. 'I think it will be great. I wanted to go…'). This helps to show their range of language. There is good vocabulary, and sometimes the student has been ambitious (e.g. 'a well-known show'; '…make my day!'). The writing isn't always totally correct, but errors are often above the level of the text (e.g. 'many **prizes**' – this word should be 'awards', but the meaning is clear).

5 / 5

Total marks: 20 / 20

This is a very strong response to the question. The reader of the email would be fully informed and would have all the information they need. The student shows a good level of language and is very accurate. The tone is appropriate for an email to the student's teacher.

Student Response B

Hi!

It's so great that we can plan a trip for our class to go to the National Theatre to have a tour next month! It will be really interesting and helpful because I like theatre a lot.

Is good to go at either time to see the show but in the pm at 2.30 is better. We can have the tour in am and have lunch after. Then we can see the wonderful show with tickets. My friend, she tell me that this show is very nice and I want to see it so much!

love

Lola

This opening is more suitable for an email to a friend than to a teacher. It is better to open the email with 'Dear...' like Student A has done.

The student has made some basic errors with language. It is important to check your writing to look for mistakes like this missing subject.

The student has used a lot of exclamation marks in their email, and this means that they stop having an impact.

The last point in the notes isn't included, so the student hasn't covered all of the required content.

Remember, you must cover all four content points in the notes. You can tick them off on the question paper as you cover them to make sure that you don't forget anything.

Text type 1: Email

Content

The content that is included is all relevant. The student has covered the first three notes. However, they haven't asked the teacher a question as the fourth note asked them to. Therefore, the task hasn't been completed and the student can't get full marks for this criterion.

3 / 5

Communicative achievement

The email communicates with the teacher but not completely appropriately. Some parts are too informal, including the opening and the closing. This is more suitable for an email to a friend. The overuse of exclamation marks also doesn't help here. To get good marks for communication, it's important to remember who you are writing to.

3 / 5

Organisation

The email has two paragraphs and there is some other organisation, such as using 'and' and 'but'. This is quite simple, and as the student has copied a lot of the sentences from the question they haven't been able to show the examiner their skill in this area very much.

3 / 5

Language

The student has copied quite a lot of the text from the question email. It is important to try to use your own words. Where the student has used their own words, there are some errors and some expressions that aren't quite right. However, the email can be understood, and these errors don't stop the reader getting the message.

3 / 5

Total marks: 12 / 20

This response is placed in the middle of the marks available. Most, but not all of the content points are included. The student could have scored better if they had included everything. The reader would not have all the information they need to be informed. The fact that the student has copied so much content from the question means that there is less of their own language to make a judgement on.

Now have a go at writing a response to this question yourself.

Read this email from your English teacher and the notes you have made.

> **From:** Mrs Jenkins
> **Subject:** Class 9B trip
>
> I am planning a trip for our class to the National Theatre to have a tour next month.
>
> I think it will be really interesting and helpful for your studies. I hope you think so too.
>
> The theatre has said we can have tickets for one of their shows too, which is very kind of them. We can see their show 'The Seasons' either in the afternoon at 2.30pm or the evening at 7.30pm. Which time do you think is best?
>
> If you have any questions or if there is any further details you need, please let me know.
>
> Mrs Jenkins

Great! (next to first paragraph)

Yes, because... (next to second paragraph)

Say which and why (next to the show times paragraph)

Ask Mrs Jenkins (next to the final paragraph)

Write your **email** to Mrs Jenkins using **all the notes**.

Highlight or underline the important words.

Outline plan:

Refer to the Planning Guide on page 14 for guidance on how to plan your response.

Text type 1: Email

Write your response (about 100 words).

☑ ☒

☐ Does your response cover all of the content points in the task?

☐ Is your response in the right style for the task type?

☐ Have you used the right register for the task?

☐ Have you used paragraphs to separate different ideas?

☐ Have you used linking devices correctly?

☐ Have you got a range of linking devices?

☐ Are all tenses correct?

☐ Have you used articles with nouns where needed?

☐ Are the prepositions correct?

☐ What about errors you've made in the past?

Email # 2

Let's now look at another email question. **Remember:**

- You must include all four points from the notes.
- Think about how to use your own words instead of the words in the question email.
- Make sure that you identify the person the email is being written for.
- Think about how formal or informal your email should be.

Read the following question. **Think about:**

- what you could do with friends on a day out.
- how to tell Alex that you are excited.
- what else you need to think about for the last note.

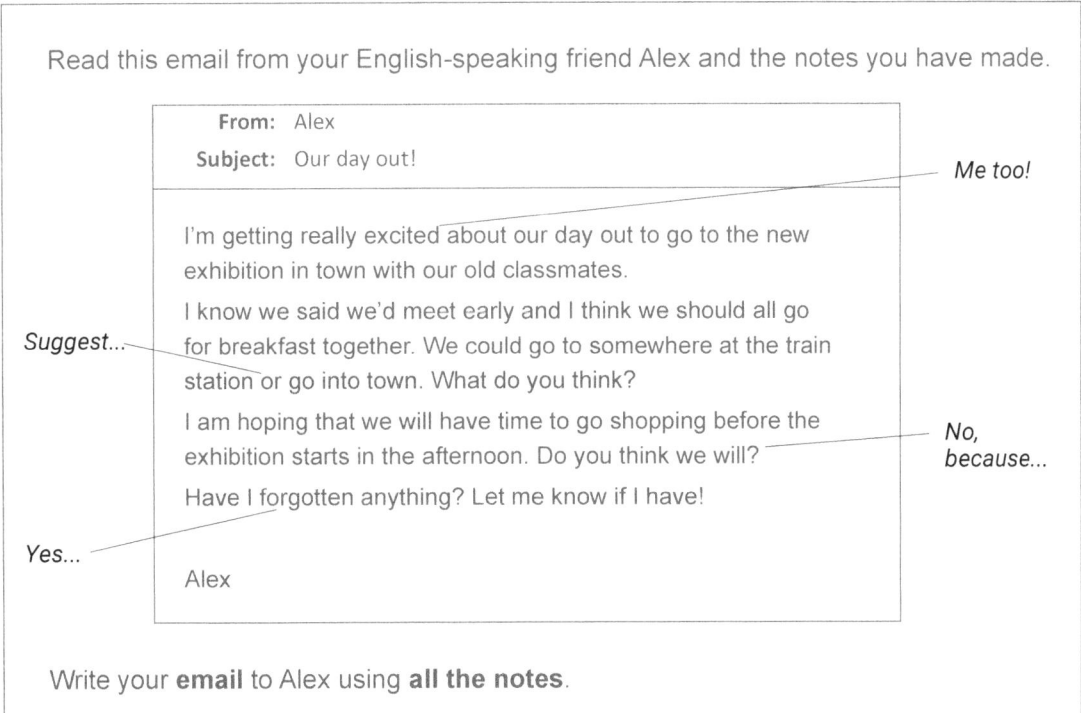

Read this email from your English-speaking friend Alex and the notes you have made.

From: Alex
Subject: Our day out!

I'm getting really excited about our day out to go to the new exhibition in town with our old classmates.
I know we said we'd meet early and I think we should all go for breakfast together. We could go to somewhere at the train station or go into town. What do you think?
I am hoping that we will have time to go shopping before the exhibition starts in the afternoon. Do you think we will?
Have I forgotten anything? Let me know if I have!

Alex

Me too!
Suggest...
No, because...
Yes...

Write your **email** to Alex using **all the notes**.

Read the following sample answers and see how two students have answered this task.

Student Response A

Hi Alex,

I am looking forward to our day out too. It's so exciting to see you all again after so long time.

It's a good idea to have breakfast together. I will leave home very early so I'll be hungry, I am sure! Let's have breakfast at the station. There is a small café there and they give a discount for students. We can save some money before our holidays!

I think it will be busy in town as it's a Saturday and there will be many people at the shops. If we go shopping, may be we will be late for the exhibition. So I don't think it is a good idea to go shopping. And I don't like to carry heavy bags.

Don't forget to give me your mobile phone number so I can call to you if I am late!

Tom

The student has used a good multi-word verb here to open the email. This is a useful verb to learn and is useful to think about using in email tasks.

The student has expanded on this point well, providing a reason for why it is a good idea to go for breakfast.

The student has made an error here – this should be one word ('maybe'), but you don't need to write perfect English to get good marks.

The email has very clear paragraphing, which helps the reader to see each point clearly.

This is a logical point to use for the last note, and it also completes the email well.

Text type 1: Email

Content

All of the content in the email is relevant to the task, and the student has covered all of the notes. They have expanded on these, sometimes in a very natural way, and the reader would be fully informed. For example, they say where they want to have breakfast, and say why they think this is a good idea and how they can save money.

5 / 5

Communicative achievement

The student has written a good email that communicates very clearly. They start well by showing that they are excited about the trip, and they communicate their ideas about all of the points. The tone is friendly and suitable for writing to a friend.

5 / 5

Organisation

The organisation of this email is excellent. There are clear paragraphs for each idea, and the student has used grammar well to join ideas up (e.g. 'If we go shopping, may be we will be late for the exhibition.' – this is very natural and makes the email easy to read). They have also used linking words to join ideas in some places (e.g. 'I think it will be busy in town **as** it's a Saturday **and** there will be many people at the shops.').

5 / 5

Language

The student has written well, and the grammar used is good. They have used conditional sentences (e.g. 'I can call to you if I am late…'), different tenses (e.g. 'I think it will be busy…') and modal verbs (e.g. 'we can save some money…'). The vocabulary is appropriate for the email and the topic, but it could be stronger.

4 / 5

Total marks: 19 / 20

This is a strong email, and the student has thought carefully about how to write appropriately to their friend. The email is well organised, and the student has very good control of language. The grammar is varied, and with some more interesting vocabulary the student would have scored full marks.

Student Response B

Hi Alex,

It's going to be great to meet you for our day out. I can't wait to see everyone again.

I think we should go to the town for to have eat. Is more place to go and we can chose better place – maybe go to where we go last time. We have some time but no enogt to go shopping. You no forgetten anything.

Jack

This is a good opening, and it is suitable for an email replying to a friend

This is a very good phrase, and the student has used it well here.

There is some organisation here as the student has used paragraphs, but the email is very short so there aren't many opportunities for the student to show that they can organise their writing well.

This email is very short at just 67 words. The questions are written to provide enough information for around 100 words, so, if you have written fewer words, check that you haven't missed something.

Text type 1: Email

Content

The email doesn't fully cover all of the required information. Although the student includes the first three notes, the content is generally very short. This is enough content, but, for higher marks, the student could have added more. They have misunderstood the last note. The note in the question says 'Yes...' about Alex forgetting something, and this note hasn't been covered in the email.

3 / 5

Communicative achievement

The student starts their email well with a good opening. However, very short sentences in the second paragraph make it quite hard to read. The email ends quite suddenly. The student could have used some more words to sign off with something that would have made it sound more friendly.

2 / 5

Organisation

There is some organisation as the student has used paragraphs, but they are very short. In Paragraph 2 they could have used some linking words to join ideas (e.g. joining the first and second sentences with 'because'). Generally, the text is too short for the student to be able to show much linking though.

2 / 5

Language

In this email, the student has tried to use their own words, and they haven't copied a lot of language from the question. Some of the opening language is accurate, but Paragraph 2 uses very simple grammar and vocabulary. There are quite a few basic errors here too (e.g. plurals: '..more place to go…') and spelling errors with words that are provided in the question (e.g. 'forgetten').

2 / 5

Total marks: 9 / 20

The fact that the email is under the word length makes it hard for the student to score well for this email. They should have used all of the words available to try to show their language skill. The language is usually simple, and the errors they have made are basic. The short sentences in Paragraph 2 make the email sound unfriendly, and this doesn't communicate well.

B1 Writing | Cambridge Masterclass

Now have a go at writing a response to this question yourself.

Read this email from your English-speaking friend Alex and the notes you have made.

From: Alex
Subject: Our day out! — *Me too!*

I'm getting really excited about our day out to go to the new exhibition in town with our old classmates.

Suggest... — I know we said we'd meet early and I think we should all go for breakfast together. We could go to somewhere at the train station or go into town. What do you think?

I am hoping that we will have time to go shopping before the exhibition starts in the afternoon. Do you think we will? — *No, because...*

Yes... — Have I forgotten anything? Let me know if I have!

Alex

Write your **email** to Alex using **all the notes**.

Highlight or underline the important words.

Outline plan:

Refer to the Planning Guide on page 14 for guidance on how to plan your response.

Write your response (about 100 words).

✔	✘	
☐		Does your response cover all of the content points in the task?
☐		Is your response in the right style for the task type?
☐		Have you used the right register for the task?
☐		Have you used paragraphs to separate different ideas?
☐		Have you used linking devices correctly?
☐		Have you got a range of linking devices?
☐		Are all tenses correct?
☐		Have you used articles with nouns where needed?
☐		Are the prepositions correct?
☐		What about errors you've made in the past?

B1 Preliminary Writing

Text type 2: Article

In Part 1 of the Writing paper you have the option to write an article.

Remember:

- An article is usually written for an English-language website or magazine.
- A heading may be useful to make people want to read your article.
- Try to make your article interesting to read.
- You don't have to tell the truth!

Look at the following question. **Think about:**

- what vocabulary you know that is connected with shopping
- what experience you can include
- what language you know for giving your opinion about something.

You see this notice on an English-language website.

> **ARTICLES WANTED!**
>
> **SHOPPING** – love it or hate it?
> Write an article telling us what you think.
> Is it better to buy things online or to visit shops?
> Where is the best place to go shopping near you?
>
> The best articles will be published on our website.

Write your **article**.

Read the following sample answers and see how two students have answered this task.

Student Response A

Shopping? I hate it!

All of my friends want to go shopping – all the time! I find it so annoying. I like to spend my time with them and going out to have something to eat and drink is fun. However, if you say the word 'shopping', I will not want to go. NEVER!

Why? For many reasons. Firstly, I think it is boring and my feet don't like walking around lots and lots of shops, to look at lots and lots of things which I can't buy. That is my second point. I don't have money. As student, we don't have enough money and I can't buy it.

When I must go to shopping, I do it online. It is faster and soon I can have my things without going out of my home. I think it's the best idea. Try it!

This is a simple heading, but it is strong and would attract attention.

This is a good way to link ideas across paragraphs.

Usually, we would try to avoid using the same words or phrases, but the student has used 'lots and lots' twice in this sentence and it helps to give the effect that she doesn't like shopping.

The student has missed the article here ('As student…'). Overall, the writing is very accurate, but make sure to check your work carefully for small errors like this.

The short phrase to end the article is very effective. Like the heading, it communicates well, and this can be a good way to end an article.

Text type 2: Article

Content

The article fully covers all of the points in the question and has a very clear focus. The reader would know exactly how the student feels about shopping. The fact that the student doesn't like shopping has given them plenty to say.

5 / 5

Communicative achievement

The tone of the article is very good. The title helps with this, and the reader would be able to tell before they start reading what sort of article it will be. At the end of the article, the student addresses the reader directly with 'Try it!', by making a suggestion. Overall, the article communicates well with the reader and has a suitable tone.

5 / 5

Organisation

The paragraphing is suitable in the article, and paragraphs 1 and 2 are linked well. The student uses grammar to link ideas. There are some short sentences that have a strong effect. In other cases, linking words aren't used, for example at the end of Paragraph 2. The article is still well organised though.

4 / 5

Language

There is a good range of grammar used in the article, such as conditional sentences (e.g. '…if you say the word shopping, I will not want to go…') and modal verbs (e.g. 'when I must go to shopping…'), and good use of the gerund (e.g. '…without going…'). The vocabulary is less strong. There aren't errors, but the student could have used more interesting vocabulary connected to shopping.

4 / 5

Total marks: 18 / 20

This is a very good article, and it answers the question very well. Its communication is also a strength. The article feels personal, and the student addresses the reader directly. The student has good control over the language used, and is usually accurate. They could have included some higher-level vocabulary though. Overall, this is a strong article.

Student Response B

Shopping

It is so funny to go shopping but I only like to go alone. It's not lonely. I can pass a good time doing the window shopping. May be you like it too? Is a good way to pass time with spend no money, no?

Shops

My favourite shop is called 'Miranda'. Is only in my country and many youngs go there at the weekend when we no have the school and like but if I go to the city there are more shops to shop and sometimes I can buy many things.

The heading tells the reader what the article is going to be about, but it is very simple.

The student should have said 'spend' here instead of 'pass'. This could be because the phrase is different in their own language. Be careful not to translate such phrases into English – they could be similar but might not have the same meaning.

The student tries to communicate with the reader of the article here. However, there are errors in the language.

This final sentence is very long. The student has used linking words to join ideas, but it is too long and this makes it hard to read.

Not all of the content is included, and the article ends quite suddenly. Maybe the student ran out of time and didn't finish their article. Make sure that you plan your time carefully in the exam.

Text type 2: Article

Content

The article covers most of the points in the question. The student talks about shopping and which shops they don't like to go to, but doesn't say anything about online shopping. This might mean that they don't like online shopping, but they don't tell us. For full marks they should have included something about this.

4 / 5

Communicative achievement

The student has some good points and some that are less good here. They talk to the reader in Paragraph 1, which is positive. This sets a good tone for the article. However, the way the article is set out with two very simple headings makes it seem less interesting, so the reader may not be encouraged to read the article. With better layout and headings this would have got higher marks.

3 / 5

Organisation

There are two clear paragraphs, but the student hasn't joined up their ideas very well. In Paragraph 1 there could be more use of linking words. In addition, in Paragraph 2 there is just one very long sentence, and this makes it hard to read. Making this two sentences would have improved the article here.

2 / 5

Language

The student generally uses everyday vocabulary here. Sometimes, using different words would make the writing more interesting to read (e.g. 'there are more shops to shop' would read better as '…there are more places to shop…'). Some simple grammar is accurate, but there are also lots of errors. The errors don't stop you understanding the meaning, but some are basic.

3 / 5

Total marks: 12 / 20

Although the student has covered most of the points in the question, the reader would not be fully informed. The content is communicated, and the reader would understand the ideas in the article. However, the poor organisation in Paragraph 2 and the errors in the grammar make it quite hard to read.

Now have a go at writing a response to this question yourself.

You see this notice on an English-language website.

ARTICLES WANTED!

SHOPPING – love it or hate it?
Write an article telling us what you think.
Is it better to buy things online or to visit shops?
Where is the best place to go shopping near you?

The best articles will be published on our website.

Write your **article**.

Highlight or underline the important words.

Outline plan:

Refer to the Planning Guide on page 14 for guidance on how to plan your response.

Text type 2: Article

Write your response (about 100 words).

✔	✘	
☐		Does your response cover all of the content points in the task?
☐		Is your response in the right style for the task type?
☐		Have you used the right register for the task?
☐		Have you used paragraphs to separate different ideas?
☐		Have you used linking devices correctly?
☐		Have you got a range of linking devices?
☐		Are all tenses correct?
☐		Have you used articles with nouns where needed?
☐		Are the prepositions correct?
☐		What about errors you've made in the past?

Article # 2

Let's now look at another article question.

Remember:

- An article is usually written for an English-language website or magazine.
- A heading may be useful to make people want to read your article.
- Try to make your article interesting to read.
- You don't have to tell the truth!

Read the following question.

Think about:

- a hobby that you know well
- what vocabulary you know that is connected to this hobby
- the past tenses that you will need for the second question.

You see this notice on an English-language website.

> **ARTICLES WANTED!**
>
> Do you have an interesting hobby?
> When did you start this hobby?
> Why do you enjoy it?
>
> We will put the best articles on the website next month.

Write your **article**.

Read the following sample answers and see how two students have answered this task.

Student Response A

Cake?

Yes – you can see from this I like to bake cakes. I started baking cakes when I was a child and my grandmother taught me. Maybe you think it isn't an exciting hobby but I like to do something to calm me after a long day of study. I love to give my friends a cake made by me on their birthday. In my opinion, everybody loves something made for them, don't they? I think it shows love for them.

Last year I entered a competition at my college for baking cakes. There were many amazing cakes. And guess what? I won the first prize! Everyone loved my cake and the judges told me I should start a cake shop. But no…I like to have cake baking as my hobby! I want to have fun with it.

So, would you like some cake?

The student uses good vocabulary here. They could have said 'make cakes', but 'bake' is a more interesting word to use.

The use of the pronoun 'them' here and at the end of the paragraph means that the student doesn't have to repeat the word 'friends'. This helps with the organisation of the article.

All of the content from the question is covered in the opening paragraph, so the student has space to move on to new ideas.

Using a personal example makes the article interesting, and the reader can imagine the situation.

The heading and the last paragraph are very effective in communicating with the reader. They are simple but very strong ways to open and close.

Text type 2: Article

Content

The student has decided to write about baking cakes in response to the question, and this is a good example of cooking. All of the content is relevant to the question, and the student has answered all of the questions that were included in the article notice. The article has a simple heading and a good ending that links back to the heading.

5 / 5

Communicative achievement

This communicates very well, and has a tone that is suitable for an article. The student gets the attention of the reader with the title, and makes it clear what the article is going to be about. The student speaks directly to the reader (e.g. 'Maybe you think this isn't an exciting hobby…' and '...would you like some cake?'), which communicates well.

5 / 5

Organisation

The article has clear paragraphs, and the student covers all of the content for the question in Paragraph 1 and uses Paragraph 2 to give a personal example. Each paragraph has a function. The article uses some individual linking words, and is well linked by grammar too (e.g. 'I started baking cakes when I was a child and my grandmother taught me…').

5 / 5

Language

The language used is very strong. There are examples of different tenses as well as difficult structures (e.g. '…started baking…'; '…like to do something to calm…'; '…a cake made by me…'). There is also some good vocabulary (e.g. 'judges'; 'have fun with it'). The student writes very accurately and has a good control of language.

5 / 5

Total marks: 20 / 20

This is a very good response to the question. It would have a very positive effect on the target reader, and they would want to read the article. All of the areas of assessment score full marks, and the student has thought carefully about how they can cover all parts of the question and still write an interesting article.

Student Response B

Run! Click!

You think this may be no a hobby but I love Two thing at a same time. My job and work is very busy and sometimes my manager she say that I have to stay later than five oclock to help with some Work that is not my Work. I Lote but is for futur very Necesary so I musted to do very mush. In today is mush peoples that has the same promlem and is very import that we has a way to Relax ourselfs I think. Some peoples don't have hobby and so can be no Relaxing all the time. I say to you, Is import to find some times to do things to relaxing. If no relax them, Maybe will be Sick and go to hospsuital for better. So we must find a nice hobby now to not do this!

This heading is good, and it suggests that the article is going to be about running and taking photographs.

The student uses capital letters incorrectly a number of times in the article. This may seem like something unimportant, but it confuses the reader as capital letters are generally used for the names of things.

It isn't clear what the student is trying to say here, and so the reader would be very confused.

The article is quite long at 145 words, and it doesn't feel as if the student has read the question carefully or planned their article.

Text type 2: Article

Content

It seems, from the heading, that the student has understood the question, and the reader would think that this article is going to be about running or photography, or both. This gets the reader's attention, but the rest of the article is very general. It doesn't fully answer the question, even though it is about hobbies. In fact, it isn't clear what the student's hobby is.

2 / 5

Communicative achievement

This article doesn't communicate well. It is quite hard to read as the ideas don't really relate to the question, and so the reader would be confused. The student includes personal opinion and experience, but in a different way to the first response to this question. It isn't focused on the topic well enough, and the response here doesn't read like an article.

1 / 5

Organisation

There is some organisation here, but the lack of paragraphing and the incorrect use of capital letters make this hard to read. It is difficult to follow the meaning overall, and sentences are not well linked in the text.

2 / 5

Language

Although there are some examples of accurate language, they are short (e.g. 'I have to stay later than…'; '…we must find a nice hobby…'). Every sentence has errors and some are basic, including some spelling errors with simple words (e.g. 'oclock'; 'mush'; 'promlem'). There is one sentence in particular where it is hard to work out the meaning (e.g. 'I Lote but is for futur very Necesary so I musted to do very mush.').

2 / 5

Total marks: 7 / 20

This is a weak response to the question. The student hasn't answered the points in the notice for the article, so the reader would be confused, but the student also does not show the level of accuracy expected at this level. They haven't considered the organisation of the article and the tone to use for the reader well enough.

Now have a go at writing a response to this question yourself.

You see this notice on an English-language website.

ARTICLES WANTED!

Do you have an interesting hobby?
When did you start this hobby?
Why do you enjoy it?

We will put the best articles on the website next month.

Write your **article**.

Highlight or underline the important words.

Outline plan:

Refer to the Planning Guide on page 14 for guidance on how to plan your response.

Text type 2: Article

Write your response (about 100 words).

✔	✘	
☐		Does your response cover all of the content points in the task?
☐		Is your response in the right style for the task type?
☐		Have you used the right register for the task?
☐		Have you used paragraphs to separate different ideas?
☐		Have you used linking devices correctly?
☐		Have you got a range of linking devices?
☐		Are all tenses correct?
☐		Have you used articles with nouns where needed?
☐		Are the prepositions correct?
☐		What about errors you've made in the past?

Text type 3: Story

B1 Preliminary Writing

In Part 1 of the Writing paper you have the option to write a story.

Remember:

- Use the sentence given in the question to begin your story.
- Underline the important words that will make sure your story fits with this sentence.
- Make sure that your story links to the idea in the question.
- Don't make your story too complicated – you only have about 100 words.
- Use past tenses (past simple, past continuous and past perfect).
- Make sure that you check your pronouns in the story.

Look at the following question.

Think about:

- the different past tenses that you can use
- the time phrases that you can include to link ideas
- any good vocabulary that links with being near a mountain.

Your English teacher has asked you to write a story.

Your story must begin with this sentence:

Jan thought the mountain didn't look too far away.

Write your **story**.

Read the following sample answers and see how two students have answered this task.

Student Response A

Jan thought the mountain didn't look too far away. She knew he could make it. She started walking on foot. It was so hot and didn't have any water. She walked and walked. The sun was shining and she didn't feel well.

Then suddenly she saw him!

A massive lion appeared by Jan. She shook in fear. She said "no! Please don't eat me!" She didn't believe it. But he didn't chase Jan. He was friendly and just sat quietly next to her. She sighed but she wanted to get to the mountain because it was safe there.

In the end, She was so surprised when the lion showed her a short cut. She will never forget that lion.

The student has correctly used the past continuous here to give background to their story.

This short sentence gets the reader's attention and makes them want to read more.

This word adds drama to the story. It is more extreme than saying the lion was 'big', and it shows the student's vocabulary well.

The student mentions the mountain again, which helps to link back to the start of the story

The student uses this phrase well to show that the story is coming to an end.

Text type 3: Story

Content

The student starts their story with the sentence from the question, and the story follows on well from this. The story is logical, and there is a further reference made to the mountain. There are a number of short sentences in the opening paragraph that help to build the story and add detail.

5 / 5

Communicative achievement

The reader would be able to understand the story on the whole. Some of Paragraph 2 could be clearer (e.g. it isn't clear what this refers to: 'She didn't believe it.'). However, it still communicates the different points in the story to the reader well.

4 / 5

Organisation

The story is organised into paragraphs, and there is some linking of ideas using 'and' and 'but' in Paragraph 3, and 'when' in the final paragraph. Some sentences aren't linked, but sometimes a string of short sentences add drama to a story so this is okay. There is a good phrase to introduce the final paragraph. Using some more linking words would have achieved a higher mark.

4 / 5

Language

The student uses some different past tenses (past simple and past continuous), and these are suitable for the story. There is also an example of direct speech used in Paragraph 2 (e.g. 'She said "no! Please don't eat me!"'). There is also some good vocabulary (e.g. 'a massive lion'; 'a short cut').

5 / 5

Total marks: 18 / 20

This is a good story, and the student has shown good control of language. They use a very good range of different language with different tenses and grammar. There are very few mistakes, and these don't stop the reader understanding the story. It has good organisation and communicates clearly.

Student Response B

Jan *thoughts* the mountain didn't look too far away. It was a nice mount and she liked to clime. Always she like to climb it. It is hard work and she sweet a lot but in the end she was done it. *She* won the gold medle! I knew she could made it and she was. She is winning the medle after so much time of try. The people at the olimpic games were *crazy with excitement* and they have a big party with lots of music. I think this day is the best day in she's live. She family are very happy she win gold medle and lots of money.

The student has made a mistake in copying the sentence from the question here. Make sure to check this when you write a story.

This could have been a new paragraph. It would make the story easier to read as this is the start of a new part of the story.

This is a good phrase, and is suitable for the story.

The story may seem strange as it moves from a mountain not too far away to the Olympic Games. However, there is a link as the student has decided that this mountain was part of an event at the Olympics. It doesn't matter that this isn't true!

Text type 3: Story

Content

The student has used the sentence from the question to start their story. The story is quite different from the story written by Student A, but this is fine. You can make your story about anything as long as it links to the sentence provided in the question.

5 / 5

Communicative achievement

The reader would be able to follow the story and would understand what has happened. The very short sentences make it more difficult, though, to read. This story is different to the Student A response where short sentences were used to add drama. Linking some ideas together would make it easier to read.

3 / 5

Organisation

The ideas in the story are connected, and the reader can see what the links are. However, the student didn't use many linking words to show this. The organisation would be better with more linking words and some paragraphing to split up ideas. This would make it easier for the reader.

3 / 5

Language

The student starts writing in the past simple, and this is good for a story. However, they make a lot of mistakes with tenses, and sometimes use the present simple or continuous in error. They use some good vocabulary, but make some spelling mistakes with it (e.g. 'mount'; 'clime'; 'medle'; 'sweet'). These mistakes don't stop the reader understanding the story, but they are noticeable.

2 / 5

Total marks: 13 / 20

While the story starts with the sentence from the question, it is sometimes hard to follow as there are lots of errors, particularly in tenses. Some errors are below the B1 level, particularly errors with spelling. There could be better organisation too, which would help the reader.

B1 Writing | Cambridge Masterclass

Now have a go at writing a response to this question yourself.

Your English teacher has asked you to write a story.

Your story must begin with this sentence:

Jan thought the mountain didn't look too far away.

Write your **story**.

Highlight or underline the important words.

Outline plan:

Refer to the Planning Guide on page 14 for guidance on how to plan your response.

Write your response (about 100 words).

✔	✘	
☐		Does your response cover all of the content points in the task?
☐		Is your response in the right style for the task type?
☐		Have you used the right register for the task?
☐		Have you used paragraphs to separate different ideas?
☐		Have you used linking devices correctly?
☐		Have you got a range of linking devices?
☐		Are all tenses correct?
☐		Have you used articles with nouns where needed?
☐		Are the prepositions correct?
☐		What about errors you've made in the past?

Story # 2

Let's now look at another story question.

Remember:

- Use the sentence given in the question to begin your story.
- Underline the important words that will make sure your story fits with this sentence.
- Make sure that your story links to the idea in the question.
- Don't make your story too complicated – you only have about 100 words.
- Use past tenses (past simple, past continuous and past perfect).
- Make sure that you check your pronouns in the story.

Read the following question.

Think about:

- where the key could be in this story
- what you might do with the key
- any good vocabulary that links with finding something.

> Your English teacher has asked you to write a story.
>
> Your story must begin with this sentence:
>
> *Kate saw a gold key in the grass and she picked it up.*
>
> Write your **story**.

Read the following sample answers and see how two students have answered this task.

Student Response A

Kate saw a gold key in the grass and she picked it up. When she saw the key, she was walking to school. But she knew she could do something more exciting!

It was a key to a special box in the bank. She went straight to the bank and they let her open the box. She was so shocked when she found the box was full of gold coins. She felt shaky but she checked and no body was watching. She grabbed the gold and she ran.

Now Kate bought a big house with the gold and has a good life. But sometimes she feels scared that she has the money from a criminal!

This sentence shows variety in the use of tenses, with the past simple and past continuous used accurately.

The box the student is referring to here has a name – 'safety deposit box'. The student didn't know this name, but has described it simply to allow the idea to be included in the story. This demonstrates good language skills.

This is a good word to use, and shows that the student understands that the word has a connotation – in other words, that it is linked with negative feelings. This helps to convey the feeling to the reader.

The student has ended the story very well with a strong final sentence that adds drama to the story.

Text type 3: Story

Content

The student has used the sentence given in the question, and the story follows on from this very well. All of the content is relevant, and there is a logic to the story. It is complete and includes some detail so it very strong for content. In fact, the student has been quite ambitious in telling this story in just over 100 words.

5 / 5

Communicative achievement

The story is communicated well. The reader would understand everything and would be able to follow what was happening. The language the student has chosen holds the reader's attention, and they communicate their ideas clearly. In particular, the vocabulary choices help with this, with words such as 'shaky' and 'grabbed'.

5 / 5

Organisation

There is good organisation with paragraphs used effectively to break the story up. Sometimes the student uses complex sentences to link ideas (e.g. 'But sometimes she feels scared that she has the money from a criminal!'). In Paragraph 2 the student could have varied the language more for full marks. There are four sentences that start with 'She...'.

4 / 5

Language

The student uses a range of different language, such as past simple and past continuous tenses, very well (e.g. 'When she saw the key, she was walking to school.'), and other grammar (e.g. '…she feels scared that…'). The vocabulary is not always very complex, but it is accurate and suitable for the story.

5 / 5

Total marks: 19 / 20

The reader of this story would be fully informed and would be able to follow it easily. It has good organisation, and the language is used very accurately. The student has shown a good language level, and there are no noticeable mistakes. With some more work on the use of pronouns, this would have scored full marks.

Student Response B

Kate saw a gold key in the grass and she picked it up. She goes to work but no with happy. She no like my work. She am ask at her work is you okay? and everyone is okay. They like they work. Kate, no.

Kate goes to the park and have a nice day. She buys some foods and some drinks. She has a picnick. She call to her frends to come with she. They come to park. They talk very much and they have a nice time. In the evening is very cold and so she goes to house and she frends with she. She buy some pizza and we have party at house. It is a very nice day!

The sentence given in the question is in the past tense, but the student has mistakenly continued the story in the present simple.

The question mark in the middle of the sentence here makes the story hard to read and is confusing.

Using short sentences can be a good way to show drama in a story. However, here there are too many errors and this makes it less effective.

A new paragraph here would help to show the change in time.

The pronouns in the story have many errors, and in this sentence it is confusing for the reader who may not be able to follow the story because of this.

Text type 3: Story

Content

The story starts with the prompt sentence, so there is an attempt at the task. However, the story doesn't mention the key again. There is a reference to the park that links a little bit to the opening sentence where the student mentions 'grass'. Overall, the student hasn't kept the story close enough to the information in the question.

2 / 5

Communicative achievement

It is quite hard for the reader to follow the storyline here. The problems with tenses contribute to this confusion too. The reader could wonder what has happened to the key, and so may be confused. The story communicates some ideas but in quite a simple way.

2 / 5

Organisation

There are two paragraphs and there is an attempt at using these to organise ideas. The ideas in the text are connected using basic linking words – usually 'and' is used. Some sentences are short and could have been connected better.

3 / 5

Language

Some simple language is correct, and there is some basic vocabulary that is appropriate for the story. However, there are many mistakes. Although these don't stop the reader understanding the ideas, they are basic and sometimes the reader may have to read parts twice to make sure of meaning. The tenses in particular have a lot of errors, and so do the pronouns (e.g. 'you'; 'she'; 'her').

2 / 5

Total marks: 9 / 20

The student has not shown a good control of language overall, and there are lots of mistakes. This has meant that they haven't been able to communicate the ideas in their story clearly. The reader would not be able to follow the story easily, particularly as it moves away from the opening sentence.

B1 Writing | Cambridge Masterclass

Now have a go at writing a response to this question yourself.

Your English teacher has asked you to write a story.

Your story must begin with this sentence:

Kate saw a gold key in the grass and she picked it up.

Write your **story**.

Highlight or underline the important words.

Outline plan:

Refer to the Planning Guide on page 14 for guidance on how to plan your response.

Write your response (about 100 words).

B1 Writing | Cambridge Masterclass

✔ ✖	
☐	Does your response cover all of the content points in the task?
☐	Is your response in the right style for the task type?
☐	Have you used the right register for the task?
☐	Have you used paragraphs to separate different ideas?
☐	Have you used linking devices correctly?
☐	Have you got a range of linking devices?
☐	Are all tenses correct?
☐	Have you used articles with nouns where needed?
☐	Are the prepositions correct?
☐	What about errors you've made in the past?

Practice tests

Test 1 | p.67

Test 2 | p.77

Test 3 | p.87

Test 4 | p.97

Cambridge B1 Preliminary Writing

Practice test 1

Part 1

You must answer this question.
Write your answer in about 100 words on the answer sheet.

Question 1

Read this email from your English-speaking friend Tom and the notes you have made.

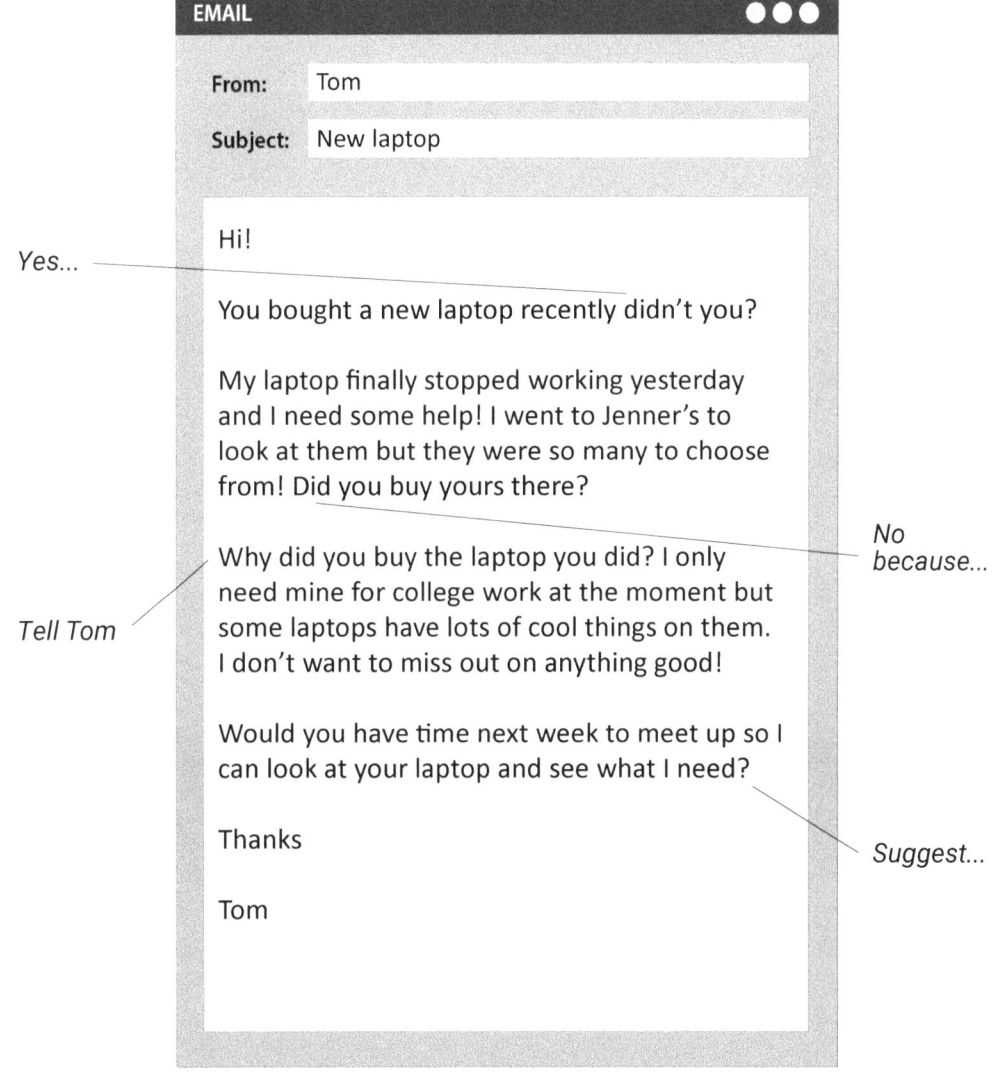

Write your **email** to Tom using **all the notes**.

Planning page

Answer sheet

Question 1

Part 2

Choose one of these questions.
Write your answer in about 100 words on the answer sheet.

Question 2

You see this notice on an English-language website.

Articles wanted!

What do you do to keep healthy?

Is thinking about what you eat more important than
how much you exercise?
What are your recommendations for keeping healthy?

The best articles will be published on our website in our
health feature next month.

Write your **article**.

Question 3

Your English teacher has asked you to write a story.

Your story must begin with this sentence:

Jack opened the envelope slowly and smiled.

Write your **story**.

Planning page

Answer sheet

☐ **Question 2** ☐ **Question 3**

Cambridge B1 Preliminary Writing

Practice test 2

Part 1

You must answer this question.
Write your answer in about 100 words on the answer sheet.

Question 1

Read this email from your teacher and the notes you have made.

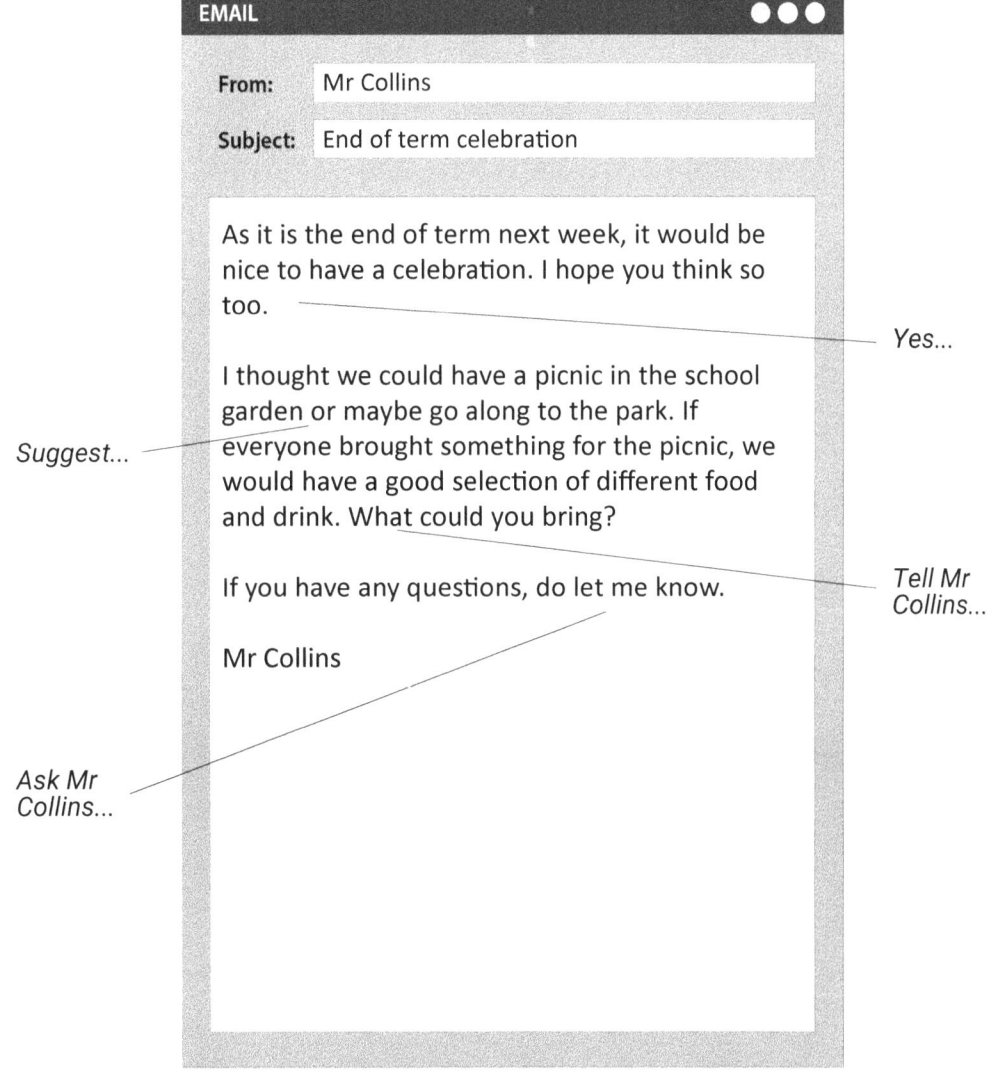

Write your **email** to Mr Collins using **all the notes**.

Planning page

Answer sheet

Question 1

Part 2

Choose one of these questions.
Write your answer in about 100 words on the answer sheet.

Question 2

You see this notice on an English-language website.

> **Articles wanted!**
>
> **Next month is travel month on our website!**
>
> We are looking for articles about great places to visit.
> Tell us where you recommend in your area and why our readers should go there.
>
> The best articles will be published on our website.

Write your **article**.

Question 3

Your English teacher has asked you to write a story.

Your story must begin with this sentence:

Sally knew it was early but she got up anyway.

Write your **story**.

Planning page

Answer sheet

☐ **Question 2** ☐ **Question 3**

Cambridge B1 Preliminary Writing

Practice test 3

Part 1

You must answer this question.
Write your answer in about 100 words on the answer sheet.

Question 1

Read this email from your English-speaking friend Jo and the notes you have made.

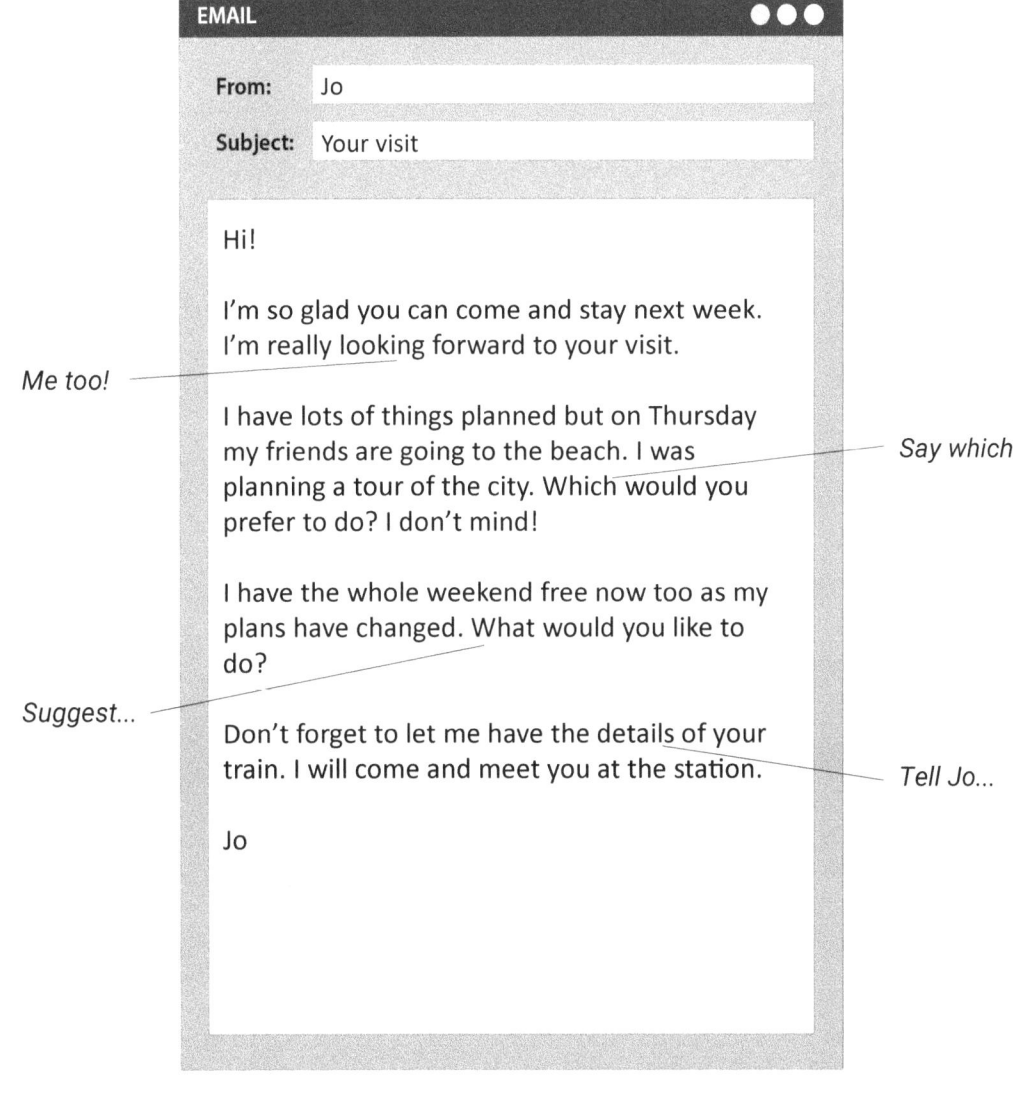

Write your **email** to Jo using **all the notes**.

Planning page

Answer sheet

Question 1

Part 2

Choose one of these questions.
Write your answer in about 100 words on the answer sheet.

Question 2

You see this notice on an English-language website.

Articles wanted!

Going to the movies?

Are you a fan of movies?

Do you prefer to see movies in a cinema or to watch them at home?

We are looking for articles for our website – tell us what you think.

The best articles will be published on our website.

Write your **article**.

Question 3

Your English teacher has asked you to write a story.

Your story must begin with this sentence:

Angela ran down the road after the car.

Write your **story**.

Planning page

Answer sheet

☐ **Question 2** ☐ **Question 3**

Cambridge B1 Preliminary Writing

Practice test 4

Part 1

You must answer this question.
Write your answer in about 100 words on the answer sheet.

Question 1

Read this email from your teacher and the notes you have made.

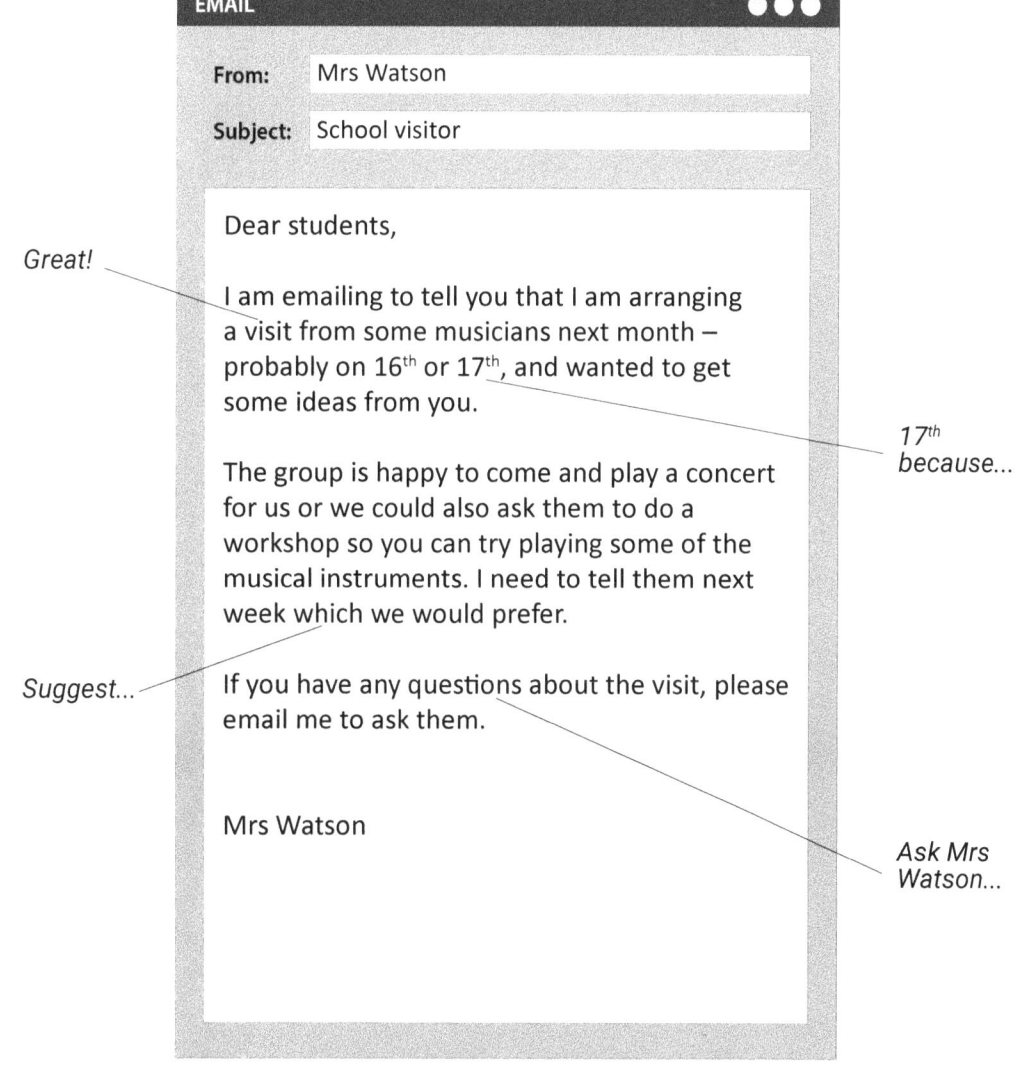

Write your **email** to Mrs Watson using **all the notes**.

Planning page

Answer sheet

Question 1

Part 2

Choose one of these questions.
Write your answer in about 100 words on the answer sheet.

Question 2

You see this notice on an English-language website.

Articles wanted!

School memories!

We are looking for articles about your earliest memories of school.
Do you remember your first day? What was the best thing?
Tell us all about it!

The best articles will be published on our website.

Write your **article**.

Question 3

Your English teacher has asked you to write a story.

Your story must begin with this sentence:

Michael stopped and realised he was completely lost.

Write your **story**.

Planning page

Answer sheet

☐ **Question 2** ☐ **Question 3**

Find more Cambridge English exam-practice resources at
www.prosperityeducation.net

www.ingramcontent.com/pod-product-compliance
Lightning Source LLC
Chambersburg PA
CBHW051316110526
44590CB00031B/4376